GOVERNOR

by Jacqueline Laks Gorman

Reading consultant: Susan Nations, M.Ed., author/literacy coach/consultant

Please visit our web site at: **www.earlyliteracy.cc**
**For a free color catalog describing Weekly Reader® Early Learning Library's
list of high-quality books, call 1-877-445-5824 (USA) or 1-800-387-3178 (Canada).
Weekly Reader® Early Learning Library's fax: (414) 336-0164.**

Library of Congress Cataloging-in-Publication Data available upon request from publisher.
Fax (414) 336-0157 for the attention of the Publishing Records Department.

ISBN 0-8368-4567-6 (lib. bdg.)
ISBN 0-8368-4574-9 (softcover)

This edition first published in 2005 by
Weekly Reader® Early Learning Library
330 West Olive Street, Suite 100
Milwaukee, WI 53212 USA

Editor: Barbara Kiely Miller
Cover and layout design: Melissa Valuch
Photo research: Diane Laska-Swanke

Photo credits: Cover, title, © Chris Kleponis/AFP/Getty Images; p. 5 © Bill Greenblatt/Getty Images;
p. 6 © David J. Phillip-Pool/Getty Images; p. 7 © North Wind Picture Archives; p. 9 © Getty Images;
p. 10 © Tim Boyle/Getty Images; p. 11 © David McNew/Getty Images; p. 12 © Barbara Laing/Time & Life
Pictures/Getty Images; p. 13 © Mike Fiala/Getty Images; p. 15 © Henry Grossman/Time & Life Pictures/
Getty Images; p. 16 © Diana Walker/Getty Images; p. 17 © Shelly Katz/Time & Life Pictures/Getty Images;
p. 19 © Hulton Archive/Getty Images; p. 20 © Bill Foley/Time & Life Pictures/Getty Images; p. 21 © Steve
Liss/Time & Life Pictures/Getty Images

Printed in the United States of America

1 2 3 4 5 6 7 8 9 09 08 07 06 05

Cover Photo: Christine Todd Whitman was the governor of New Jersey from 1994
to 2000. She was the first woman to serve as governor of that state.

TABLE OF CONTENTS

CHAPTER 1

Who Are Governors?

The United States is made up of fifty states. Each state has its own government. Each state also has its own governor. A governor is in charge of the state government.

The government of each state is split into three parts. The governor and his or her helpers form one part. The other two parts of the government pass the laws and rule on the laws.

Bob Holden was the governor of Missouri in 2001. He gave a speech about the state.

The governor is the leader of the state. He or she meets with the president of the United States and others on behalf of the state. The governor visits other countries for his or her state.

A hurricane hit Florida in 2004. Governor Jeb Bush met with people who had to leave their homes.

The governor works in the capital city. He or she has an office in the state capitol building. Most governors live in their capital cities, too. Some live in special houses. Others live in their own homes.

Augusta is the capital city of Maine. The state government offices have been in Maine's capitol building since 1832.

CHAPTER 2

What Does a Governor Do?

State governments have many roles. They keep law and order. They watch over business. They take care of the environment. They also help run the schools. Governors make sure that all these things work well.

The citizens of a state elect many people in the state government. The governor picks many others who work for the state. He or she may also pick some of the top judges in the state.

George Ryan (*left*) was governor of Illinois in 2001. He helped fill sand bags in a town where there was a flood.

Governor Rod Blagojevich (*center*) of Illinois signed a bill into law. Members of the state legislature watched nearby.

Each state has a group of people who make up the legislature. The people in the legislature pass new laws. New laws are called bills. The bills go to the governor. The governor signs the bills.

The governor may not like a bill. He or she does not have to sign it. Then the legislature can vote on the bill again. The bill becomes a law only if enough people vote for it the second time.

Arnold Schwarzenegger (*center*) is the governor of California. He celebrated after voters approved his plans for the state.

Frank Keating visited a building that was bombed by terrorists in Oklahoma City in 1995. He was the governor of Oklahoma at the time.

Governors make sure that people keep the laws. Some governors can ask for special meetings of the legislature. They decide how to fix problems at the meetings. Some governors also head the military and state police who protect the people in the state.

Governors travel on business for their states. They may visit other states. They may even go to other countries. They try to get other countries to buy things made in their states.

Governor Gary Locke of Washington visited China. He climbed up the Great Wall of China. He is the first Chinese-American to be elected governor of a U.S. state.

CHAPTER 3

How Does a Person Get to Be a Governor?

The adult citizens of a state elect the governor. In most states, they vote for the governor every four years. The people in New Hampshire and Vermont vote for a governor every two years.

In some states, a person can be governor as many times as the people want. In other states, someone can only serve as governor twice, or for two **terms**.

Ella Grasso was the first woman elected governor of Connecticut. She served as governor from 1974 until 1980.

Bill Clinton was the governor of Arkansas. He was one of the youngest governors in U.S. history. He later became president of the United States.

In many states, the governor must be at least thirty years old. He or she must have lived in the state for a certain number of years. These rules are not the same in every state.

People who want to be governor travel all over the state. They talk to voters. They give speeches. People all over the state vote on Election Day. One candidate gets the most votes. He or she is elected governor.

Ann Richards of Texas ran for governor in 1990. She was elected.

CHAPTER 4

Famous Governors

Many governors became president. Franklin
Roosevelt and Jimmy Carter were governors.
Ronald Reagan, Bill Clinton, and George W. Bush
were, too. Each one later became president.

Many states have had fine governors. Sam Houston was governor of Texas in the 1800s. He did great things for Texas. Bob La Follette was governor of Wisconsin in the early 1900s. He had exciting new ideas that moved his state forward.

"Fighting Bob" La Follette was the governor of Wisconsin from 1901 to 1906. He helped his state with his new ideas.

Thomas E. Dewey was governor of New York from 1943 to 1955. He made things better for the people of New York. Mario Cuomo was governor of New York from 1983 to 1995. He made things better, too. The people in New York received good schools, hospitals, and roads.

Mario Cuomo was governor of New York for more than ten years. He made things better for his state.

In 1990, Douglas Wilder made history. He was elected governor of Virginia. He became the first African American to be elected governor. Wilder served in office for four years.

In 1990, Douglas Wilder of Virginia became the first African American to be elected governor. He ran for president in 1992, too. He did not win.

Glossary

capital — the city where a state or country's government is located

capitol building — the building where government offices are located. The legislature meets in the capitol building.

citizens — official members of a country who are given certain rights, such as voting and freedom of speech. Citizens also have duties, such as paying taxes.

elect — to choose someone for a government office by voting

legislature — the part of a government that makes the laws. The legislature is elected by the people.

terms — specific periods of time that people serve in office

For More Information

Books

Being a Governor. A True Book (series). Sarah De Capua (Children's Press)

State Government. Kaleidoscope: Government (series). Suzanne Levert (Benchmark Books)

The State Governor. First Facts: Our Government (series). Mary Firestone (Capstone Press)

Web Sites

FirstGov for Kids–State Websites
www.kids.gov/k_states.htm
Find information about your state and its governor

National Governors Association
www.nga.org/governors
All about United States governors and their states

Index

About the Author

Jacqueline Laks Gorman is a writer and editor. She grew up in New York City. She has worked on many kinds of books and has written several children's series. She lives with her husband, David, and children, Colin and Caitlin, in DeKalb, Illinois. She always votes in every election.